Dad's Journal
My Untold Story

Section one
The Beginning

Section two
Family history

Section three
Childhood years

Section four
Teenage years

Section five
When I was..

Section six
Parenthood

Section seven
More about me!

Section eight
Final notes

No part of this book may be scanned, reproduced or distributed in any printed or electronic form without the prior permission of the author or publisher.

Copyright 2021 - The Life Graduate Publishing Group and Romney Nelson

We love to receive reviews from our customers. If you had the opportunity to provide a review we would greatly appreciate it.
Thank you!

A Place to Share My Life Memories.

Dad xx

"Of all the titles I've been privileged to have, 'Dad' has always been the best."
- Ken Norton -

THE BEGINNING...

Baby Dad

MY INTRODUCTION

Before I start....just a brief introduction about me!

_____
_____
_____
_____
_____
_____
_____
_____
_____

Name:

Signature

Date

THE BEGINNING.....

Full Name at Birth
___

Date of Birth   /   /
___

Time of Birth   :
___

Day of the week you were born?
___

Height at birth? (if known)
___

Weight at birth? (If known)
___

Your Place of Birth (include the City/Town, Country)
___

Did you have any siblings when you were born? If so, what were their names and their ages?
___
___
___

ADD ANY ADDITIONAL NOTES OR INFORMATION HERE...

THE BEGINNING.....

Share with us some information about your parents?

_____
_____
_____
_____

Were you in good health as a baby?

_____
_____
_____

Did you have any unique characteristics or funny things you did as a baby?

_____
_____
_____
_____

IF YOU HAVE ANY EARLY BABY PHOTOS, INCLUDE THEM HERE...

THE BEGINNING.....

Were you an active or quiet baby?
_____

Were you ever told what your first words were?
_____
_____

Do you have any other baby memories to share?
_____
_____
_____
_____
_____
_____
_____

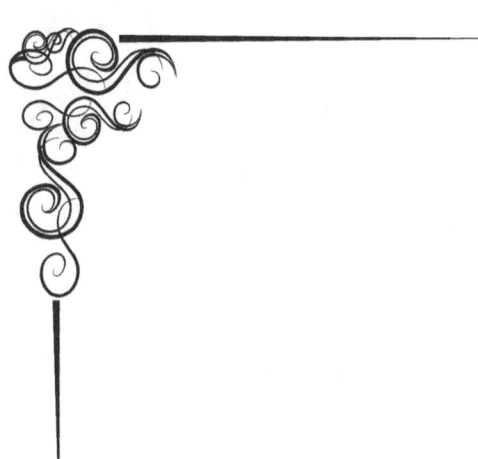

"Every father should remember one day his son or daughter will follow his example, not his advice."
— Charles Kettering -

FAMILY HISTORY

This is our Family Tree!

FAMILY HISTORY

My grandparents names were:

Grandmother (Fathers Side): _____

Grandfather (Fathers Side) _____

Grandmother (Mothers Side): _____

Grandfather (Mothers Side) _____

They were born in: (country)

Grandmother (Fathers Side): _____

Grandfather (Fathers Side) _____

Grandmother (Mothers Side): _____

Grandfather (Mothers Side) _____

This is something that not many people may know about our family history……

_____

_____

Additional Family History information:

_____

_____

_____

Our FAMILY TREE

Grandfather

Grandfather

Grandmother

Grandmother

Mother

Father

Me

ADD ANY ADDITIONAL NOTES OR INFORMATION HERE...

CHILDHOOD YEARS

CHILDHOOD YEARS....

What was your favorite toy growing up?

_____

_____

Did you have a pet or any pets growing up?

_____

_____

What was your favorite T.V show to watch as a child?

_____

_____

Was there a moment you remember getting into big trouble as a child? Was there a punishment?

_____

_____

_____

_____

ADD ANY ADDITIONAL NOTES OR INFORMATION HERE...

CHILDHOOD YEARS....

What are your fondest memories growing up between the ages of 5 - 12 years?

_____
_____
_____
_____
_____
_____
_____
_____
_____
_____
_____
_____
_____

IF YOU HAVE ANY EARLY CHILDHOOD PHOTOS, PLACE THEM HERE...

CHILDHOOD YEARS....

What was your favorite meal as a child?

_____

What elementary/primary school did you attend and where was it located?

_____

_____

Describe your most memorable moment or story from elementary/primary school.

_____

_____

_____

_____

_____

_____

_____

CHILDHOOD YEARS....

Where did you grow up as a child?
(house, location, town etc)

___

___

___

___

Who was your best friend or your best friends as a child?

___

___

___

What was your favorite day of the week and why?

___

___

___

___

___

DO YOU HAVE ANY SCHOOL PHOTOS, OR OTHER DETAILS TO SHARE?

TEENAGE YEARS

TEENAGE YEARS....

Describe your dress sense and clothing as a teenager. Is there anything that stands out for you?

_____

_____

_____

When and where did you learn to drive a vehicle?

_____

_____

What was your first vehicle and how much did you purchase it for? Tell us your special 'first car' story!

_____

_____

_____

_____

_____

_____

_____

INCLUE ANY 'FIRST VEHICLE' PHOTOS OR OTHER INFORMATION HERE..

TEENAGE YEARS....

What High School did you attend and where was it located?

_____

_____

Who was you favorite teacher or coach and why?

_____

_____

What was your favorite subject at school?

_____

_____

Did you date anyone at High School?

_____

_____

_____

SHARE ANY FURTHER DETAILS HERE

TEENAGE YEARS....

What hobbies did you have as a teenager?

_____
_____
_____

What is your most memorable moment as a teenager?

_____
_____
_____
_____

If you knew what you know today, what would you have done differently as a teenager?

_____
_____
_____
_____

SHARE ANY OTHER DETAILS OR MEMORIES HERE

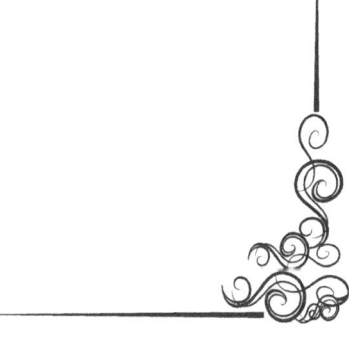

TEENAGE YEARS....

Did you have a close friendship group? Have you maintained contact with any of them?

_____

_____

_____

_____

Did you have any nicknames at High School?

_____

_____

What 5 words come to mind to describe your teenage years?
1. _____
2. _____
3. _____
4. _____
5. _____

WHEN I WAS..

WHEN I WAS....

When I was a child, my mode of transport to school was..
_____

_____

When I was in my teens, the biggest news story that I recall was .....
_____

_____

_____

When I was growing up, my 3 favorite movies were:

1. _____
2. _____
3. _____

WHEN I WAS....

When I was a child, the first movie I went to the theatre to see was..

_____

When I graduated from elementary/primary school, the year was..

_____

When I was a child, I wanted to be a......

_____

When I was 18 years old, my favorite music and band was..

_____

When I was in my teens, the most popular thing to do on a Saturday night was.......

_____

_____

When I was young, I loved to travel to.......

_____

_____

_____

SHARE ANY FURTHER TRAVEL MEMORIES HERE..

PARENTHOOD

PARENTHOOD....

How old were you when you first became a parent?

_____

Explain how you felt emotionally when you became a parent for the first time?

_____
_____
_____
_____
_____
_____

Where were you located (city/town/country) when you had your first child?

_____
_____
_____

SHARE SOME PARENTING PHOTOS HERE..

PARENTHOOD....

What has been the biggest challenge for you as a parent?
_____
_____
_____
_____

What are 3 key responsibilities you believe are important as a parent?

1 _____

2 _____

3 _____

PARENTHOOD....

Who were the first visitors you had when you had your child/children?

___

___

___

___

___

___

EXPAND ON ANY FURTHER PARENTING MEMORIES YOU MAY LIKE TO SHARE

___

___

___

___

___

___

_____

_____

_____

_____

_____

_____

_____

_____

_____

"The quality of a father can be seen in the goals, dreams and aspirations he sets not only for himself, but for his family."
— Reed Markham

MORE ABOUT ME!

MORE ABOUT ME....

Not many people know this about me, so let me share it with you:

_____

_____

_____

_____

_____

_____

_____

The activity or hobby that I enjoy most to do now is.....

_____

_____

I have the unique ability to be able to....

_____

_____

_____

MORE ABOUT ME....

If I was able to go back to a special time in history, it would be...
___
___
___

If I could pass on one word of advice to others, it would be..
___
___
___

There are special moments in life that you wish you could pause to enjoy for longer. Mine would be......
___
___
___
___
___

MORE ABOUT ME....

I wish I had the opportunity to...

_____

_____

_____

The quote that resonates most with me is..

_____

_____

_____

My favorite book of all time is:

_____

If there is one thing I would like to be remembered for it would be:

_____

_____

_____

_____

MORE ABOUT ME....

When I look back on my life so far, my 3 proudest moments are:

1 _____

2 _____

3 _____

If there were 3 famous people that I could invite for dinner they would be:

1 _____

2 _____

3 _____

MORE ABOUT ME....

From my teen years, these are the jobs that I've had:

___

MORE ABOUT ME....

One of the jobs that stands out as my most enjoyable has been..
___
___

The most interesting place I have ever traveled to has been.... (include the year/date this occurred)
___
___
___

If I was given a free return flight to anywhere in the world, I would visit...(include your 'Why')
___
___
___
___

SOME EXTRA SPACE FOR INFORMATION OR PHOTOS HERE..

FINAL NOTES

FINAL NOTES....

There have been many questions that I have answered in this book, but I would also like to share this with you...

Your time to write anything else you wish to share...

FINAL NOTES....

FINAL NOTES....

FINAL NOTES....

USE THE FOLLOWING PAGES FOR CERTIFICATES, AWARDS. PHOTO'S ETC..

THANK YOU FOR SHARING YOUR LIFE STORY

This book was created by
Romney Nelson

OTHER BOOKS
BY
The Life Graduate Publishing Group